Why Me?

– PETE HOPWOOD –

An environmentally friendly book printed and bound in England by
www.printondemand-worldwide.com

Mixed Sources
Product group from well-managed forests, and other controlled sources
www.fsc.org Cert no. TT-COC-002641
© 1996 Forest Stewardship Council

PEFC Certified
This product is from sustainably managed forests and controlled sources
www.pefc.org
PEFC/16-33-415

This book is made entirely of chain-of-custody materials

Pete Hopwood

FastPrint Publishing

www.fast-print.net/store.php

Why Me?

All characters are fictional.
Any similarity to any actual person is purely coincidental.

A catalogue record for this book is available from the British Library

ISBN 978-178035-740-9

First published 2013 by
FASTPRINT PUBLISHING
Peterborough, England.

ACKNOWLEDGEMENT

Joyce Brotherton
Sleaford Writers Group
Coningsby Library
Emma Cross
Jan Spooner
John Elliot
Hayley Clarke

CONTENTS

A KID'S LIFE
A day in the life of a young lad

The alarm clock goes off at 6:45am. You turn it off, have a yawn and wipe the sleep out of your eyes. Trying to be quiet and not to wake anyone, you find your clothes on the floor beside your bed. Getting out of your jimjam bottoms, then getting dressed in the bathroom, still trying to keep quiet. Going downstairs to the fridge, you have a glass of milk then on go your socks, shoes and coat. Outside you jump on your bicycle and off you go. About ten minutes later you arrive at the shop where you pick up the papers you will be delivering. As it is a Saturday you get paid £1.50. Not bad as you are thinking what to buy.

Off you go on your round and halfway round you see a milkman doing his delivery. It is not unusual to see him a few times during the week. 'Borrowing' a pint when he is delivering to houses, you put it in the bottom of your bag. You wait to ask if he wants you to take a couple of pints to one address, if he will take papers to another, saves both of you about five minutes. A little further on you stop and drink your 'borrowed' milk and leave the bottle with other empty bottles at someone's house.

By the time you finish your round it is 8am. When you get home everyone is still in bed. You look at your paper to see the football fixtures and who your team are playing. You have a bowl of cornflakes for your breakfast, and then you decide what you are going to do.

Your mum is getting up and you say that you are going for a bike ride to such and such a place and will be back about 1:00pm.

"Make sure you are!" is the reply. "And don't forget to tell someone."

Off you go with your two bob in your pocket for ice cream or sweets; Saturdays are usually a sandwich or a bag of chips from the chip shop.

You meet a friend at his house and he wants to come as well. Same thing with his parents, "Don't be late!" Pedalling away you know it will be a little hard as there are steep hills to cycle up and down. With having five-speed racing bikes you only find one hill a bit too much, so you push the bike up as you go to your destination. The weather is good, sunny with a little breeze. Both enjoying your trip, you arrive at your destination after forty minutes. It is only about six miles from home but to you it is like being on holiday. You are at a picnic area; there is a parking space, shop, toilets, café and a river. Bikes put down outside the shop, in you go for a bag of sweets or a chocolate bar.

A few other families turn up, some in cars, not many, and others on the bus. All the kids seem to get together like a magnet with iron filings, everyone looks after everyone else.

After running around for a while, a dip in the river to cool down is the order of the day. No one cares, every one of the kids who goes for a paddle strips off to their underpants or knickers, After all, kids are kids, and no one thinks it rude, naughty, or about some older people getting a kick out of it. After a while everyone leaves the river and goes back to their own, to get dried and changed. You and your friend just take off your wet pants and put your trousers, T-shirt, socks and shoes on and put the wet pants in the saddlebag, say your goodbyes off you go to get home. You know that you have the steep hill going down this time and with the wind in your hair you try to go as fast as you can. On arriving home it is to the pantry and grab a couple of slices of bread to make a jam sandwich.

Now you are back, you find your mum to let her know you have returned and are off to the football match. It is only your local town playing the town about 10 miles away in the local league. A few of your schoolmates turn up, you all enter the ground and go to the same place you go to for every home game, right behind the goal. When the opposition come out, all the boos are heard, then the cheers when the home team follow. Normal chanting goes on through the game then, shock, your team let in a goal. You shout at your team to do something quickly. Half time comes and so does the pie man; at least it is a warm pie today, usually they are cold.

The second half starts and the cheers seem to never stop as your team are putting a lot of attacks on the opposing goal. Then everyone goes mad, an equaliser, brilliant, twenty minutes left to play and to score a winner. The crowd are behind the team, the team respond with another goal, home fans including you are ecstatic. At the final whistle your team win 2-1, you are happy. Off you stroll home to get the other football scores. Your team in the main Football League Division 1 have drawn. They didn't get beaten, that's all you care about.

Having a quick bite to eat you go outside to play with the rest of the kids in the street. You can stay out until it gets dark. Playing tag, hide-and-seek or football depending on how many there are. Your mum and dad are going out, as they do every Saturday, for a game of bingo and a dance. You then come in and watch TV; as it is a Saturday you can watch *Match of the Day*. It finishes, you switch off the TV and go to bed.

Not bad for the day in the life of a young lad. I know that because that young lad was me.

SEPARATED
Always together, then split

From the earliest of memory we had been together, never left each other's side. Everything was done together; if one was cold, both were cold. The same if it was hot. We did a lot of travelling on lots of different types of transport, some were fast and some slow, but always arrived at our destination.

The different things we did together were incredible; the cornflakes at breakfast in summer and the porridge during winter. Tea and coffee, *Horlicks* or chocolate drinks we made, perfect. Cakes and biscuits were also something we helped with. Even the pet cat was happy when we came in.

But like everything disaster struck. We found out that separation was on the cards. There was nothing we could do about it, we were not in control. Nothing we did would change the situation. Off we went to the place where we would both go our separate way. Would it be hard to leave, being together for so long and then nothing?

When separated we were near each other but could not get back together as we used to be.

After all, I was a fresh pint of milk that had now gone sour and separated.

A MEMORY NEVER FORGOTTEN
The truth is in the seeing

Working thousands of miles away from home seems not a good idea. But near the equator, and also with time off to do what you want, now seems a good thing. For six months your job takes you into a hot climate that you are not used to. A suntan, because of your red hair, will cause a bit of a problem, but do you care? No chance. Sun factor whatever is available, but do you use it? On hot days back home you didn't put on anything to protect you, you just went red and if it was a bit too long, you knew about it later.

When you arrive, the first thing that hits you when you leave the aeroplane is the dry heat. Your jumper is off even before you get to the bottom of the stairs and onto the tarmac. Sweat starts to appear on your forehead and everyone is asked not to open bags for towels or hankies to dry themselves because something may drop and cause FOD (Foreign Object Debris).

After customs and passport checks, you are met by the person you are going to replace. After introduction, they take you to your place of work to meet the rest of your workmates. In the next couple of hours you find out where you will be staying and everywhere else you may need to go. After lunch you and the person leaving take one of the company vehicles on a tour of the local area. When on your time off, and if it is your turn to use the vehicle, you can visit anywhere in your own time. Not realising what you have been doing, window down, arm out of the window, your arm is red, deep red and it is a bit sore. So on your first day the calamine lotion is used to ease the pain. After a few weeks you are going around in shorts, T-shirt and flip flops, but you had taken your time. At first you wore jeans and a T-shirt, shorts only for work. You did a bit of sunbathing – ten minutes each side one day for a week, then added a couple of minutes every week for the first month. Now it's swimming trunks, shorts, T-shirt and towel as the meeting place was the swimming pool. You could now take the heat, but not for hours on end.

One day the shift was finished and it was your turn to have the vehicle, so after a change of clothes off you went. You have been told of a place that has a small secluded beach, but you have to obey the sign. Not knowing what to expect, off you went. With the temperature about 90°F and a little wind, everything was fine. Arriving at the car park, there was one other van there. Looking around there was only one path and all you could see was a hut, grass and the sea. You were on the top of a cliff and the beach was below. You couldn't see it, but could hear the waves breaking. Going down the path you saw the sign. All it said was *Shout Male/Female coming and wait a couple of seconds before setting off.* You think, what the heck and shout, "Male coming!" wait, then carry on. About twenty yards further on another sign exactly the same as before, obeying the instruction you shout again. About ten yards further and you can see the beach, water and this hut. Another few yards and the last steps to the beach are at the side of this hut. Never having been there before you didn't have a clue what it was or why it was there. Arriving on the beach a couple were there and said hello and thanks.

Being naïve, you asked, "Why the thanks?"

"You did shout at both signs didn't you?"

You answer, "Yes. Well, it's my first time here and I was told to obey them but didn't know why."

Their answer was simple, as the beach was so secluded and couldn't be seen until you were nearly on it, both males and females found it the best place for privacy to sunbath topless or nude. With shouting, those on the beach had time to cover up and no embarrassment would be caused. Genius idea.

You ask the couple what the building was (the hut).

"It was a lifeboat hut from the late 1890s to 1910."

From where the beach was now to the hut, it would be impossible to launch now as the sea was about ten metres below the small runway for the boat. "Could anyone have a look inside?"

"No, it is condemned and has been since it closed when the crew of the lifeboat all died. No one knows exactly why they all died within months of each other and all from the same disease. Their graves are a little further along the path."

At 2:35pm the couple say their goodbyes and leave. Being curious you decide to look for the graveyard. Along the path you go, and you are met with what looks like two white pillars of stone embedded in the hillside. On entering it looks just like an oval room with the walls all round, from the floor going up and out for about twenty feet, then the sky. It was strange, there was a small pathway around with graves on the outside and about four on the inside. The wooden headstones were worn but names could be read on some, dates on others and some were in a bad condition, but there was one on each grave.

It was then you noticed, when you looked up, there wasn't a cloud in the sky. How or why? Because you knew when you were travelling there, there were clouds. A little further and another observation came. There was no grass, weeds or any plant life, just stones to mark the pathway and the sandy dusty soil. How was this, as the rest of the island had grass all over? Looking at a few of the graves, you found a couple of the fallen lifeboatmen were only seventeen or eighteen years old. What could they have died from? After a little thought you realised how quiet it was. You couldn't hear the sea yet you were only yards away. There wasn't even a slight breeze, everything was ironically dead. It felt eerie, looked eerie and by yourself you were pleased it was daylight.

When you came out, literally about five yards past the white pillars, you heard the waves, felt the breeze and saw the grass and birds. By the time you reached the hut, only thirty yards away, everything seemed the same. Well, that visit must have taken about ten or fifteen minutes, or so you thought. Going back to the vehicle, you know you arrived at 2pm and the couple left at 2:35pm, so it should be about 3pm. The van clock read 3:50pm. How did you spend over an hour in a graveyard, yet it seemed only minutes? What had taken you to stay that long? Or was it just the thought of trying to understand the reason of why it was completely different atmosphere outside and yet even time in the graveyard was dead? EERIE!

Arriving back to the work compound, you were asked if you had been to the beach and seen the graveyard. Saying yes and then telling of your feelings about the place, everyone else came out with the same sort of memory after their first visit. But did say you have to go again.

"Why?" you ask.

"You will find out in your own way," was the reply.

The next time you went to the graveyard you knew what to expect but it was still quiet and peaceful. The difference was you felt just as strange as the first time. You still felt as if you were being watched by someone or something. You didn't touch anything or move a stone. You still thought of how they died and from what. You felt at peace there. Nothing moving, no noise, no nothing.

You cannot put it into words but everyone who visited the graveyard all said the same. "When there, you remembered your own family who passed away, not just one, but all." Nowhere else has had that effect on so many people, that you know of. Yet everyone tells the same story, and has the same feelings after visiting the graveyard of the brave lifeboat crew.

God bless their souls.

TIME, NOW AND THEN
How did we manage?

Once upon a time in a land, when if you only had a little, you were normal. Hard work was a way of life, and love thy neighbour was just as it says.

A couple would prepare an evening meal and leave it to heat later or put it on slow cook if a stew or braised meat was the special treat. On leaving the home, a horse and cart with scrap and clothing goes past. Walking hand in hand, two children on a homemade go-cart go past. It was made with two sets of pram wheels, two short and one long plank of wood and a few nuts, bolts and brackets with string to steer.

As they walk past a playground they see a row of bicycles, girls skipping and others on a swing. A group are playing tag whilst another are kicking a tennis ball in a sort of game of football. A little further and a half-sheep and cow are hanging outside a butcher's shop, with rabbits and chickens also on show. The shop is very busy.

A small coffee shop is their destination. Meeting a few other friends just for a chat, this is their weekly thing every Friday. The ladies all stay and the gents nip next door to the pub for a pint or a half, nothing much, just a refresher.

Do they take a bus back or walk, that is their choice.

After arriving home, they have something to eat and wash and dry the dishes. After a little rest, it's Friday night pictures. Down to the Odeon cinema, they queue for a while with the other couple of hundred. Two hours later out they all come and go straight home or pop into the pub for a drink.

Move forward fifty years with the same couple looking at a young couple now.

How they would prepare their evening meal, simply open a deep freeze. What was one of them? A pantry with a cold slab was all they had.

On walking outside, about three or so dustbins on wheels. All different colours, all for different things. No one coming to their door for any recyclable things and the bin man taking everything they didn't collect. It was up to the householder to sort it out, put it in the proper bin and take the bin to the road. No friendly collector coming up the path to the house and collecting the waste and returning the bin.

Walking was a no-no. Into the car and past the school. The children are in small gangs, only a few are actually playing. It seems a break is not used to let off steam but to hang about in small groups.

Arriving at the shops, the butcher has all the meat on display under fly-free screens, with tongs and plastic gloves at the side for health and safety. All the meat is a bright red, not dark brown or white for pork, nothing is left uncovered and is all chilled.

The coffee shop is a little bakery as well, serving cakes and biscuits with drinks and background music.

When they arrive home, the 'meal' is put into a small oven-type machine for about two minutes and, ping, a hot meal. Only a couple of plates, knives and forks to wash, plenty of time to get ready for the film.

Not going out, just put the TV on. No long wait for the valves to warm up and then a black and white picture. Then a small disc put into the TV and *voilà*, the film. No trip to the cinema, no queue and no smoke-filled room. You watched the film and if you wanted to go to the toilet you just stopped the film.

Fifty years earlier it took ages for everything yet you were all healthy. Now it is all health and safety and obesity. Fifty years later still it will be the same again, everything now will be going out of date in a couple of years, let alone fifty.

How did they manage fifty years ago, when now everyone doesn't have enough time? They lived without pre-packed food, deep freezers and fridges, or foods served with tongs and gloves. Didn't have any cars, and buses were few and far between. A walk didn't kill them and there was no problem standing in a queue.

How did they survive fifty years ago? The same way they have survived for the last few hundred years.

Everyone disagrees with the next generation, saying, "You wouldn't be able to cope in my day." They disagree with the health arrangement, money problems and the cost of things and not having enough spare time.

The world will still survive no matter how much discord there is between everyone and every generation!

SOMETHING NEW
A day of doing nothing

I'm going to take my car out, I don't know where to go.
Will it be the seaside, no one else will know.
First I'll put the petrol in, and then I'll start the car.
It will not go, the battery's flat, I won't be going far.

A walk is what I'll have to do, to get me out the home.
My hair's a mess, but I don't care, I haven't got a comb.
The walk it starts so briskly, and then it starts to slow.
The body says, let's turn back, but you have to say no.

Your destination is in view, and you start to feel just grand.
Two hundred yards and you'll be there, with money in your hand.
When you get to the door, you find out it is shut.

And all you see, looking at you, is their hairy mutt.

You don't know what the problem is, you haven't got a clue.
Why can I not enter in, I don't know what to do.
And then the answer hits me, I feel just like a fool.
It's only half past ten am, eleven o'clock the rule.

The landlord opened up the door, only because it's me.
He locked the door, gave me a beer and said that one's not free.
I went to grab my money, but he said not just yet.
Some nosey parker will tell the cops and they will come, you bet.

A few come in and then they go, but you, you're going to stay.
The barman says, "Another one?" and you say, "I have all day."
A beer is just what you want, and time is no concern.
You came, you got, can have a lot, cos you've got money to burn.

The day it has all ended, and you wobble to
your feet.
The taxi's come and you go home, what are
you going to eat?
You live alone and you don't care for bread or
cheese or crisps.
But what is in the cupboard, that's the little
risk.

You wake up in the morning and your head is
banging hard.
No it is not the first time, you wonder if you've
been barred.
Your wallet it is empty, you don't know what
to do.
It's time to ask that important question, tell
me something new.

TRAPPED
What happens when you are caught?

I was feeling hungry so I made my way to the waterhole I always used, thinking what I shall have. As usual, plenty to drink but nothing to eat, not even a crumb.

Having had my fill of drink, I looked around for something else to ease my hunger. Then I could smell that smell that says, come and get me. You know, just like going past a fresh bread shop or a barbeque on the go. The smell you could not resist.

When I arrived there was no one there but the food was ready. I had a quick look around but saw no one. I knew the person wouldn't mind if I started by myself, but I thought, no wait.

After a few minutes I could not wait and thought. Sod it, go for it. As soon as I took my first bite I heard something and tried to move away out of sight. But I was too late. The man came in and smiled, after that I don't remember much.

After all the noise all I heard was a click and piece of metal locking my head.

YES I'M A MOUSE AND I'VE BEEN TRAPPED

GROWING UP, LYRICALLY
From child to OAP in song (117)

Growing up isn't easy when *All You Need Is Love.* You are a *Bad Boy* so you are told. Every time you do something you feel as if you are in *Chains* and are told *You Can't Do That.* Your life is a *Misery.* I thought as a *Little Child* it would be *Something Your Mother Should Know,* but every time you asked a question all you received back was, as a teenager, *I Should Have Known Better* and took more notice.

With space travel you have seen a monkey go into space and a dog. You wonder what else goes on *Back In The USSR.* Would you like to fly *Across The Universe* or not. Would you *Get Back,* do you like *Flying*? This could be one *Magical Mystery Tour* where we could all *Come Together* and have a *Helter-Skelter* ride. No one else will be able to *Help* you. This is your fantasy. Thinking of other things takes your mind off the normal day. You try to *Act Naturally* but you are sure that you are being watched.

Yes, growing up is hard and when you become a young man you think *Yesterday* was a good day, but today *I Feel Fine*. Young women are becoming more prominent in your life. A young girl, *Michelle*, and a group of *Boys* were at a party and *I Got A Feeling* that she was the *Girl* for me. Nothing was said or done at the beginning of the evening but later in the evening looking out over the patio, *I Saw Her Standing There* all by herself. I went to her and asked if she was all right. She said *Tell Me Why* when she tried to talk to people, all men are looking for is a one-night stand and then nothing. I replied, "Well I will talk and listen and between the *Two Of Us* we may *With A Little Help From My Friends* find out that *We Can Work It Out*."

Being friends for a couple of months *All My Loving* of her started to send me to being a lovey-dovey. I told her, "*I Want To Hold Your Hand*." She looked at me and said. "*Till There Was You* nobody cared but you treat me like a lady." She also would *Ask Me Why* I found her such a catch, I'm no *Mean Mr Mustard* and *If I Fell* in love with her would she say *Hello Goodbye*, was I just a *Ticket To Ride* or was she after my *Money*? Working all hours I seemed to work *Eight Days A Week*, but I

Want To Be Your Man and that's *From Me To You.*

There was no pushing the point of getting together, it just happened. Planning on moving in together *There's A Place* in *Penny Lane* where we could live. She said yes and that it may be a *Long And Winding Road.* Giving her a kiss that was *A Taste Of Honey* I said, "*Oh Darling, I Want You, Because, You Really Got A Hold On Me.*" Her reply, "*I Need You.*" Yes, *She Loves You*, and *I Love Her.*

Why Don't We Do a lucky dip on the lottery and buy a raffle ticket as that was the most excitement in our lives. Raffle number 910 *One After 909* our ticket number but the lucky dip came up. *Baby You're A Rich Man* was shouted *Baby It's You* who has won. Before picking up the money we both went as *Day Tripper*s to the coast. Having a drink and sitting on the beach, the clouds broke, *Here Comes The Sun* we said putting on some sun cream. Sitting together we saw a *Black Bird* as *Free As A Bird* and two *Boys* trying to *Dig a Pony* in its side with a stick. The owner said it would take a *Revolution* to stop kids being naughty, we just *Let It Be.* Another child was playing with a *Yellow Submarine* and I am sure it was made with *Norwegian Wood.*

Travelling back home we passed raspberry and *Strawberry Fields Forever.* They went for miles and all there was were field after field of pick-your-own products, we went in and by the time we had finished I thought how are we going to *Carry That Weight.* I don't know how we did it; we needed *Maxwell's Silver Hammer* to get it into the car. I then said baby you can *Drive My Car, Any Time At All* as long as you *Slow Down* and have A *Day In The Life* with *Mr Kite.*

Having had a good night's sleep (I had been in *Golden Slumbers*) when Michelle said, "*Do You Want To Know A Secret*?" "Of course," I said, "I didn't think you had *Something To Hide.*" "I have written a book and want to be a *Paperback Writer.*" "I *Dig It,*" was my reply; now with the money from the lottery we could do this. After the publication visitors to the house were unbelievable. Complete strangers who no one knew, it was an *Octopus's Garden* of bodies. You had to *Twist and Shout* just to get around or be heard. Then *I've Just Seen A Face* that you know is either going to please or destroy you. *Lovely Rita* was a stunner and had a lovely tan, she was a *Sun King* and knew it, was I going to be the *Fool On The Hill* and give everything away. Yes. Because of what was happening, others said, "*You're Going To Lose That Girl* so *You've Got To Hide Your Love Away.*" How was I going to keep on seeing Rita? After a few weeks of the two-timing I wasn't sure if anyone knew what was going on, it was so bad for Rita sometimes *She Came In Through The Bathroom Window.* Soon Michelle found out, and then the message *She's Leaving Home.* Even with money it still *Can't Buy Me Love.*

In the morning reading the problem page *Dear Prudence* a similar story was printed, *Maggie Mae* was seeing *Eleanor Rigby* but she had a crush on *Polythene Pam.* I started thinking, *I Am The Walrus* and not a *Nowhere Man.*

I had made my mind up and wrote a letter to Rita, went outside and said, "*Please Mr Postman* could you take this letter for me?" Struggling I found out I had had a few *Hard Days, Night* time was just as bad. A few days later the mail came and in the letter was the words do you *Love Me, Do* you. I had answered that in the letter I had sent. *You Never Give Me*

Your Money even if you could. When you were happy you looked like *Lucy In The Sky With Diamonds*. Looking at you I go *I, Me, Mine*, I'm so in love with Rita and still will be *When I'm Sixty-Four.*

But I knew *It Won't Be Long* before the *Taxman* would have me *Fixing A Hole* in our bank account. Everything was *Getting Better* and with *Words Of Love* my girl would *Hold Me Tight.*

With the *Rain* coming down I thought, *I'm A Loser* and with *No Reply* thought yesterday I had nothing, today everything, Yes my *Honey Pie* is happy so *Cry Baby Cry*. While she *Gently Weeps* she says *I'm So Tired* I lost everything, but not now *Not A Second Time*, and *P.S. I Love You.*

The End

YOU ARE NOT ALONE
One person's view of the universe

We are here, they are out there? This question will always be asked, until something of an *ET* situation comes about. Mind you, if someone did come and tried to say they came from a few hundred light years away, would you think that they were of sound mind, trust them, or have them taken away to be cut up for tests etc., etc.? But we are a friendly planet, so they say. You know, the experts who have sent spacecraft into the unknown, to keep on going, hoping, someone will see it and check the 'contents' of how good Earth is, where it is, and that we need an atmosphere to live. Something we know is not available on Mars.

Voyager I was sent into space in 1977 with information about our planet. The nearest planet outside our solar system is that far away the craft will not arrive for a couple of thousand YEARS. In that time, I think, this planet will have changed, just a bit, from the information on board.

Probes have gone to other planets in our solar system but as there are eight circling our sun, we are only now, 2013, getting information from ONE of these. Yes they have gasses, winds and explosions. One powerful telescope and satellites show this, but if we can only see this, how do we know something is not happening, under the surface, to help them live as they do? After all, here on Earth we can live at either +40°C or -40°C so what is wrong with someone able to live at either +2000°C or -2000°C (yes, -273°C is absolute zero, but that is here on Earth, not out there).

TV programmes try to put other planets on the same level as Earth. Why is it every planet *Dr Who* lands on has an atmosphere the same as Earth, so no masks? At least the occupant isn't the same, not human as we know man and woman, but with a skin protection for their climate.

As everyone knows, there must be something or someone else out there. Just looking at the television brings out what could be out there. Nobody expects a tin man, but the *Daleks*, they seem real. How could an advert make you change your mind, as one advert says – SIMPLES.

Outsiders looking onto Our World would say it exactly as it is, "They peel them with their metal knives, boil them for twenty of their minutes, then they smash them all to bits." How many are looking at us thinking, they can only go two or three times the speed of sound, we can go half the speed of light? It takes us about five days to reach the Moon so to an OUTSIDER we are primitive. This one advert of a tin man advertising a potato powder could be something that IS happening. Someone with a much higher intelligence, just checking that we are still not good enough to be a threat.

Do things like this happen? After all, the Boy King Tutankhamen had a pyramid built for his resting place when he died. He was ten years old when this happened. Try building one today. With all our technology and machinery of today it would take about twenty-five years. So how did they do it? Were they from another planet, landed in the Middle East, built cities, monuments etc. but when, for some reason, something happened and they 'Died'? Were they just fed up, packed their spaceship and took all of their secrets with them, maybe to another planet and are still looking down.?

It is said that from a height, somewhere in the world, there are markings that have been there for thousands of years, yet on a smaller scale it matches the runway etc. of London's Heathrow Airport. Did they have aircraft or is this just a coincidence?

Two hundred years ago the British sent prisoners to the Southern Continent – Australia - and let them fend for themselves. Given what they had, they had to survive, or die. What is wrong with another intelligence, having travelled through space, found a little planet, ours, and thought, we could send our prisoners here? Transport took months for ours to reach their destination by boat. So travelling through space, at their speed, for a couple of months, and then dropping them off to fend for themselves. No matter how good you are, or how rich you may be, if you have nothing to work with, you are just as good as the person next to you. The examples of this are, if you were a builder, chef or mechanic, the first thing you would need is food, but where is it? You will have to catch it, kill it and then cook it. With nothing to help you, you need a weapon of some sort to kill the animal. A long stick for a spear or short ones to use as a sort of knife, but don't forget, you don't have anything to make these weapons sharp! When the animal is caught and killed, it needs cooking. No matches, so two bits of wood rubbed together. It would be the same as living in prehistoric times, with a group having to work together. And with having nothing it would take hundreds of years to make very basic things.

Now two thousand years later, we are what we are now. With 'THEM' looking in, keeping us just where they want us. If we did find another life would it be the one that had sent the 'prisoners', therefore they would know we are getting a little bit closer to being as intelligent as them? Do they leave us alone or as the record sang *In the year 2525, Now it's been ten thousand years* do we let it go on or take it down and start again?

The film *Total Recall* showed that someone or something may be able to put some sort of device to make oxygen, nitrogen etc. by heating the frozen ice. This may be what is happening on other planets; so far away we can only imagine that an intelligent 'other' may have done this. Why, for future use? A lot of people think that WE are the only planet with life. Why can we not accept that there may be more out there than we think? Like a mirror image of us. When you look in the mirror is it you, you are looking at or your spitting image on another dimension, and visa versa?

As we can see at night, there are thousands of stars, but if they all have planets we will not be able to see them, therefore we would not know if any did exist. Our Sun is only nine minutes away (light speed) the next is over four years away and others hundreds of light years away. This being true! Imagine if from the furthest away they have 'died' and are not there, and coming closer they also have blown up and made black holes. We could be, in about thirty years, looking at about ten stars and the other eight planets. The reason being the light is still coming from those suns. If we sent out a light beam to see how far away other stars are in 1960 we only have twenty-seven years worth of stars we know still exist, and not the thousands everyone thinks there are (27 years for the light to travel out and the same to return).

Everyone has their own theory, films, adverts and TV programmes are someone's ideas of what is, could, or may be out there and what dangers may come if we found out. No one knows for sure. If *Mork from Ork* did come, *ET* knocked on your door, or a phone box just appeared in your back garden with the occupant just carrying a screwdriver, sorry a sonic screwdriver, what would you do? Again everyone would have their own answer. We don't know what exactly is happening out there but they may know how far we have come and are just waiting for the right time to let us know there is someone else. Earth is our world, our planet. So why not let some other life say the same of their world, their planet? This is one person who thinks this could be how it is. Just as the person who did the TV show, advert or film, everyone has their own opinion.

WHAT IS YOURS?

WHY WORRY?
A problem many men will or have suffered

The waiting is horrible. Knowing what is going to happen will eventually happen. The time, not a clue, the place – that depends. Nothing was guaranteed. There you are watching the TV wondering. It's not your favourite programme but trying to keep your mind away from the situation is very hard. No one can really help you. You brought this upon yourself, and now must face the consequence. Even work has problems. You may get a call, your presence is needed somewhere else, your workmates will most probably say – good luck, or it happens – even at the wrong time.

You have a situation, but it doesn't count, because your main problem comes first. When it does, every bone in your body, all your regrets and anything done wrong will be of no relevance. You are by yourself, no help, no information, no clue what to do.

Whilst in bed you wonder, is it now or even when you close your eyes will there be that call you have waited for to end your torment. As nothing came that night you still didn't sleep properly. Looking over your shoulder when you go to the shop, on hearing a car backfire, an emergency vehicle siren, or even someone shouting, you start sweating. Doing your shopping everyone asks are you all right. You always seem to be getting everything done quickly, as if 'it's going to happen, I want this job done'.

You try to have a quick beer, no chance. Anyone and everyone tries to calm you down, even if you don't need it. The pint you have doesn't seem to be going down, looking at the clock you then know why. Only ten minutes of what seemed hours have passed, and now you start to get yourself together. Only now do you have a chance to think out loud. After all, by yourself at home, it takes a lot to have a conversation.

Just talking to people about anything was a relief. For some reason you have a cold shiver. Is it now or not? You start sweating and then a few sips of beer to try and calm your nerves. You hear a mobile phone ringtone, it's not yours, another sign. Another day of nothing. What will tomorrow bring?

Another bad night. You feel and look terrible. A cup of coffee to try to wake you up. A quick splash of water on the face helps, but the razor stays on the shelf. You're not going to work so you have to do something. Just as you are about to start, your telephone rings, you answer in a quiet voice. The person on the other end asks if you are the person they are after. Confirming this, you are told where to go and do it now.

Putting your jacket on you leave the house and get into the car. Not waiting for any more calls you drive carefully. On arrival you are met by a man, who takes you into a room where your eyes open wide. This is something new to you. Never before have you been in this position. Five others are in the room. You start sweating, no one else. One then screams and screams and you go closer to the screams. Then quiet. The person who was screaming holds out a hand and you grab it, giving comfort then a hug.

Another comes to us and the three of us are together. No one will separate us, no matter what now the waiting has finished.

What was going to happen has. The time was later than expected. The place was expected and the final result had been perfect. Yes today has been perfect. Me, my wife and the apple of our eyes, our newborn baby.

A DREAM HOLIDAY – FOR SOME
No clubs or loud music, heaven to some

The heat hits you as soon as the doors open on the aeroplane. Jackets and jumpers are coming off already. On leaving the aircraft you get the full force of the sun. Not a cloud in the sky and you have two weeks of this. The small island has no beaches full of hotels, English pubs and food outlets.

Your four-bedroom 'hotel' is one of the biggest and a car is only needed to and from the airport. You walk everywhere. Only takes two hours to completely round the island and visit the seven beaches. All are different, small and large, golden sands and rock pools. One has a small boat which can be hired for sea fishing or just a boat trip to see the different colours of fish in the clear water.

Life on the island is normal. The 'church' is a building with three large rooms but three different insides, separate religions. One is no shoes, set times and days for each prayer time and open for visits or for you to have a private prayer. Yes, there is a pub or two but the whole island is the same as a village, except it isn't far from a beach and the sun nearly always shines. The locals know each other and with only about one hundred visitors there is not the drunken behaviour you will find on the Costas. As most visitors are over fifty and few families go, it is a place to relax, have a look around and see how others, miles away from mainland always have fresh water to drink and plenty of fresh fruit and meat.

The history of the island is in the handbook given to everyone on the plane showing places to visit. Apart from the 'church' the older part of the island has taken nothing away with houses over one hundred years old in a small circle. With a central point, where presumably meetings or meals were done, everything was basic but nothing was moved.

An island just to chill out, let your mind wander and forget about everything. Top up or get a suntan in no time. The only downside is if it rains. It will last about an hour or less, but flood the lower land. Flood drains you thought were cycle routes run like rivers. Then a couple of hours after the rains stops, dry as a bone. Going back to the airport, everyone of the villagers come to say goodbye. You have had a good time and wanted to shake everyone's hand. The plane takes off, you look back and say, "I'll be back!"

WHY ME?
One person's life turned upside down

Looking through the blinds from the darkened room, the rain pounding down and only one street light working. Washing-up not done, clothes on the floor, dust and an unmade bed. To David this was hell. Fridge full of beer, some milk and enough cheese for a sandwich. Only one knew how he lived. But who would come out of the dark? Were they after him or coming to help!

* * *

Five years earlier he could not have cared who was on the street, the sun shining, a cleaner finishing the housekeeping, David leaving in a new car to go to work. He enjoyed everyone and everything. The people, his workplace and all who worked with him. Mixing business and pleasure was part and parcel of his lifestyle. Going out for a meal or a round of golf, which he didn't really like doing, with workers and their partners was normal. Everyone paid their own share or an equal fund by everyone was paid. No one was better than anyone else. David worked with Philip, Stephen, Mick and Carol and it was then, when John joined, everything went pear-shaped.

David was a senior line manager enjoying all the pressure of work and the comradeship of the workers. He arranged events, i.e. meals out and get-togethers. Only a handful took up the invitation and the only other 'single' person was Carol. She started a couple of months earlier and because of her qualifications, was so far up the ladder and was trying to qualify for a management position. Living by herself, she had no boyfriend and kept herself to herself, but always seemed to have money.

Philip and Sandra started the same day as Carol, Philip was also a line manager, being a deputy to David he kept an eye on everything that went on and reported back any problems. He was engaged to Sandra, who worked in the Admin Department. They rented a house in the local area. It was in the better part of town, had a garden and garage, but for what they earned together, they still seemed to be living a little above their status.

Mick and his girlfriend rented a smallholding and were saving a little to either go for their own property or in case they decided to start a family. He being one of the workforce in the factory, anything that was needed to be done in that part, he would be asked to do it, pack, clean or box up etc. His partner did part-time cleaning in a local public house.

Stephen and Emma were married and Stephen fixed the machinery if it was to fail or break down, and set them ready for the worker to use. Emma, as Mick, was one of the workforce and both of them rented any property that was cheap, so moved around a little. All went out to the 'dos' David arranged to keep prices down, including house parties where the visitors took the drink and the hosts provided food.

John enjoyed all the outings at first, but soon his wife was with him, who had lived abroad for the last three months, while he set up home. She was a thirty-year-old, dark red hair with a body of an average female. Not tall and thin or short and stout, just a beautiful looking woman. Charlotte knew this and played on it. This seemed to upset a lot of the other men and their partners. Being the senior of this group, David thought it would split the social group up so a chat with John was what was needed. The belief was things would change, as Charlotte's dress sense and flirting were put to question. After a few functions had passed things seemed to be getting better. But then Sandra, Philip's fiancée, came to David with a story of betrayal because of Charlotte and Philip's affair. Sandra worked in the office next door, so was often seen walking into other departments.

How could Philip, a thirty-year-old engineer, betray a twenty-seven-year-old secretary, with whom he had been together for two years and who were perfect for each other, for a flirt whom he had known for only a month? What does a thirty-four-year-old man do when a friend's partner comes for help, when he is single and hasn't had a relationship for over three years? David listened to her story of the last function, when Philip went to help Charlotte with a problem on her mobile. Nothing seemed to happen then, but the next day he was on his phone a lot more than usual. She found out by looking on his phone whilst he was in the shower and found Charlotte's number with a text saying when they were going to meet. Sandra went to the venue and found both wining and dining and asked David what she should do. Leave Him? Ask him why, or one of the dozens of other questions that could be asked? The tears came and so came the first close hold of a woman David had had for years. Crying on his shoulder and arms locked around each other, what else could happen? After a few minutes David broke the hold and made a drink, asking if she needed anything to help. "Just a friend to talk to," was the answer. David sighed with a little relief as he didn't want to be another player in the love circle.

* * *

A few days later, another night out had been planned and David was wondering if Philip and Sandra were going to turn up, as the party was at John and Charlotte's home. Yes, was the answer. Both looked nervous and stayed well away from each other. Even during the meal they were a few places from each other but on opposite sides of the table and were in each other's eye line. Eyes were looking at both couples as it was no great secret about Charlotte's flirting with anyone, so everyone was keeping their wits about them. Nothing else happened during the meal, but you could cut the atmosphere with the bluntest of knives.

The group decided to have a game of some sort, to try to make a night of it. With four couples and two singles, David and Carol were put as captains of men-versus-woman in charades. The five men each wrote one act for the ladies and put them in a bag, therefore they didn't know what they would do for their team, and the girls did the same for the boys. The first drawn, Stephen (Emma's partner), was given an easy *ET* to do and Margaret (Mick's partner) had the song *Message in a Bottle* by The Police. It was a hard one and no one answered right from the girls which started a bit of a squabble. After all the boys had done theirs, four had been correctly answered with one wrong, and the girls had three right and one wrong, with only Charlotte to go. Philip knew what the subject was, as his was the only one not drawn out and with a smile on his face, he knew it should be easy (*The Hills have Eyes*). Up she stood and in a flash took her top off and was stood in her bra. Using her finger she went from one armpit over one breast into her cleavage, over the second breast to the other armpit, then using each hand pointed to her face towards her eyes. David asked her to put her shirt back on but she just turned to the boys showing herself in a skimpy top and looking at Philip with a smile. Emma stood up, grabbed the shirt and put it over Charlotte who pushed it away and said she wasn't ashamed of what she had. Even John, her partner, was in agreement saying we were all being prudish. Surprisingly Mick and Margaret were both in agreement, saying we were all adults and nothing was showing. You see more on a beach when on holiday, so what is the problem? Sandra looked in disgust but Philip seemed to share the opinion of the others. Emma and Stephen were just gobsmacked that it happened in someone's house, but said if everyone had known it could happen, who wouldn't have turned up? Carol and David looked at each other, shrugged shoulders and said to each other, being singles they didn't care less who showed what as long as they didn't expect everyone to become involved. Sandra put her coat on and told Philip she was going home and would he come too. Sheepishly he said yes, but went to everyone, shook the hands of Mick and Stephen and gave their partners a peck, but when he shook

John's hand he had a smile on his face and a twinkle in his eye when he gave Charlotte a full-on smacker. Carol turned her hand to him for she didn't want a kiss and David kept quiet when his hand was shaken. With one couple gone, David and Carol both made their exit.

* * *

At work the following week, everyone was looking at everyone else. Philip asked John, Mick and Stephen what happened after they left. They all said strip poker, but would not say who, if not all, ended up naked. With a smile on all their faces John said he could fiddle the cards and all the girls lost. David heard about all of this and was surprised that all the lads still managed to talk to each other, until he found out they were all swingers, and Stephen and Mick knew John from holidays they had taken and had talked together to try to bring in Philip and Sandra, to see if they would enjoy this style of life. Having done nothing wrong there wasn't a lot that could be done, except ask them to leave Philip alone and not mention this again to him. David talked to Carol about this over a drink in the local pub, it took over two hours, then surprisingly Sandra came in, saw them and asked if she could join them. There was no problem and the subject of the other night wasn't mentioned apart from Sandra saying she was still talking to Philip but had not stayed at his or him at her house since that night. She missed the company but Philip was okay going out by himself. Sandra didn't know where he went and asked if they knew would they let her know. Carol, after a couple of drinks, let it be known that she had seen Philip with Stephen and Emma in another drinking establishment and they left at about 9:30ish in Stephen's car. Knowing Philip and Stephen lived on opposite sides of the town, yet Stephen lived only about 400 yards from the establishment, why go in the car! Sandra started crying and saying he was partying with them and everything else that came to mind. Carol told her to stop thinking about it and go and do the things she wanted to do, now Philip was doing what he wanted, until they work something out.

Sandra asked for a strong drink and asked to go back to Carol's for a little privacy so the whole town wouldn't know her situation and listen in. It was only a two-minute walk to Carol's house and David agreed to walk with them. He was invited in and accepted. Drinks were poured and Sandra started on about the night of the charades and that she hadn't had more than ten words to say with Philip. He hadn't rung or even sent a letter, all she could think of was him with Charlotte. Carol gave Sandra a shoulder to cry on while David was thinking about what had happened differently at work and did that have anything to do with the situation. His mind was wandering trying to think of what happened over the last few weeks at work. Did things happen that were not true, was anything unusual or out of place? Nothing was, as far as he was concerned. Coming out of his thoughtful mind, he saw both women in a very passionate hold. Hands all over each other and a full-on kiss. How long this had been going on, David didn't know, but Carol then held out her hand toward David to bring him into their company. He accepted. There were no words spoken, hardly any noise made but slowly, very slowly, an occasional piece of clothing fell to the floor.

* * *

David woke with a beam of sunlight in his eyes. Looking around he saw he was covered with a blanket on a chair in Carol's house. He still had his boxer shorts on and the rest of his clothes were folded on the floor beside him. He dressed and looked around for someone, but nobody was where he was. He went into the kitchen, nobody, so he put water in the kettle and switched it on, before going upstairs. Looking into one bedroom, it was empty, it looked as if nobody had been in it for years, everything tidy, nothing out of place, bed dressed down, curtains exact mirror image left and right drape. Nothing on the floor, i.e. shoes or slippers. But the next bedroom was different. Toys on the window, footwear, clothing on the floor and chairs and both Sandra and Carol in bed asleep. The phone rang and woke Carol, she saw David, said hi and answered the phone which was next to her bed. After about twenty seconds she put the phone down and proceeded to get out of bed, wearing only a pair of knickers. She didn't seem bothered about David as she went to have a shower.

"Coffee?" David asked.

"Yes," was the reply.

David went to the bathroom downstairs before making three coffees on a tray with a jug of milk and a sugar bowl. He took them to the bedroom where a few noises were coming from Sandra. A few moments later, Carol returned wrapped in a towel and Sandra's eyes opened. She sat up in bed pulling the blanket up with her. David asked what happened, as he could not remember from joining them to waking up. The girls looked at each other and gave a smile.

"You felt tired so we put you to sleep on the chair and we came to bed."

Not knowing exactly what happened David had to trust them. He finished his coffee and said he was going home for a shower and change. Leaving the house he looked back when he was about twenty yards down the street, and saw Philip drive up, get out and rush into the house. Did he go back in case Sandra was in trouble or carry on home? Then Charlotte followed from the passenger side, so David carried on home. Thinking of everything that had happened, David made himself a drink, sat down and tried to think of what could be done about the way his so-called friends were behaving.

* * *

Back at Carol's, Carol, Philip, Charlotte and Sandra were communicating with each other as if nothing had happened, talking about the last few days when the door bell rang. Carol went to answer it and there was John, who seemed very excited. He went straight to Sandra, who rushed towards him and hugged and kissed him, took his coat and made him a drink. How was everyone? Philip asked. Everyone nodded their head saying everything was okay, just as expected and no problems. The conversation went rather deep, as Philip asked what was David doing there as he had seen him leave, just as he was driving to the house. Carol looked at Philip and answered everything was fine with a smile on her face. Where were Steve and Emma, Charlotte asked. They were with Mick and Margaret shopping and would be there in about two hours.

* * *

The sun was hot and there was no wind or clouds in the sky, a very peaceful day. To keep his mind, David went into his garden to do a little weeding and grass cutting, talking occasionally with his neighbours and passers-by. His morning seemed to go very quickly, then Emma and Stephen came past in the car.

How are you? David was asked. Fine, was the answer.

"We heard you took Carol and Sandra back to Carol's last night," Emma said.

"Where did you hear that from?" asked David.

"Charlotte, we have been shopping and popped into Carol's."

Suddenly David felt cold. Sandra was there, didn't like Charlotte and Philip, and was John there as well? What could happen or, worse still, what has or had happened at Carol's last night?

* * *

Days and weeks went by, nothing was said at work and the functions stopped. Everything went on as a normal day, everyone talked to each other as if they were normal workmates with nothing to hide, no back stabbing and no 'I'm better than you' attitude. David felt he had lost a few friends. He received the normal good morning, evening and bye, as well as the weather and work, but no, are we having another get-together. He went out by himself and tried to make new friends in the public houses by playing cards, dominos, darts etc.

And it also gave him a little company, rather than sitting at home looking at four walls. He soon found one young lady, whom he had noticed for the last few weeks and spoken to a couple of times, who was interested in him, his job and interests. Paula worked as a receptionist in a local golf club (one thing David knew nothing about, except you hit a ball and then spoiled a good walk). It was a well-paid job, good hours, only one weekend per month, and occasionally you could have a chance of winning a couple of tickets for one of the British golf tournaments, when the world's best would be playing. David wasn't bothered about the golf, just getting away to Scotland and Ireland cheap.

Paula and David looked as if they were meant for each other, both looked happy when together. They never stopped talking, were laughing and joking, making a fool of each other, but not upsetting the other. They both had their own places and stayed there. Visited each other's but never stayed the night, a good friendly couple, no commitment, no pressure. Everyone at David's work soon realised there was a change in his attitude to work. He was happy, enjoyed the excitement of the day, seemed to be looking brighter and more alert.

Always with a smile on his face. He was excited because he had found a relationship that had made him happy. Something that had not been part of his life for some four years, since his last girlfriend sadly passed away after a car crash.

David was happy, Paula shone when she was out with David and after three months, David asked Paula if the relationship could go to another level without spoiling what they had. Paula answered with, "We can try as long as we don't rush." Engagement, marriage and living together were no-go areas. Introduction to family came up first and both agreed. David's mum and dad lived fifty miles away and Paula's had moved to France, but also had a house in England which they commuted to. Her brother looked after the house when they were abroad.

Three months later the chance of David taking Paula to his parents came. Nothing fancy, no posh frocks, just comfortable attire. When they arrived, David's mum and dad were sitting in the back garden having a drink. On seeing their son, both stood up and made Paula very welcome, first asking if they wanted anything to drink. After all, it was a hot day and they had just driven fifty miles. David and his dad started talking men talk, and the women engaged in women talk. An hour passed then all four decided to go indoors. Everything was fine, mum and dad were very impressed with Paula and their son.

After a long weekend, David and Paula left with the best wishes of his parents. From then nearly every two or three days, David's mum would ring asking a little more about Paula and David would answer then say, "Why do you want to know that?" or "Why do you have to ask so many questions?"

Mum's answer, "I'm looking after my boy, what's wrong with that?"

It was a few months later when they went to Paula's parents and the same happened. Everyone was happy with the situation and enjoyed each other's company, no one thought that anyone was better, more privileged or higher class than the other. The perfect start to their relationship.

* * *

Over the next two years, David and Paula's relationship really took off. Nights out, holidays, they went everywhere together, did everything except work together. After their last holiday, they went to Paula's parents showing them the photos of their trip and all the other things. When David asked Paula's dad if it would be acceptable if he asked for his daughter's hand in marriage, he was delighted and said, "I hope she says yes."

A little later the question was bought forward and with a 'yes' and a kiss, Paula's mum burst into tears, she too was happy. The wedding would be in nine to twelve months, time to get everything sorted out. The next few months were hard. David had agreed to move in with Paula and rent out his house. Why have two mortgages, the rent from David's would pay his and twenty-five percent of Paula's. But what did he take from his house, what did he leave and what did he store?

Both sets of parents were communicating with each other and their siblings and everything was falling into place. Where to hold the wedding reception and honeymoon destination? How many from each side? The maid of honour was no problem for Paula, but who would David have as his Best Man? He hadn't had any real male friends over the last two years. So he asked Paula if it would be all right for him to ask his boss. It was agreed only if Paula could get to know him. With the wedding very close Paula gave David her approval of John, his boss, being the Best Man.

The day of the wedding came and Paula looked magnificent in her long flowing bridal dress and her maid of honour and bridesmaids were just as beautiful. David and John were waiting for the music to start signalling the bride's arrival. Both were sweating but as soon as his bride stood next to him, David just smiled and felt great. The ceremony passed and the photo shoot went perfectly. The sun was shining, very little wind and hardly a cloud in the sky. Even the reception, which was in a large hotel garden with a marquee, couldn't have been better. The grass was dry and the flower bed was full of blooming flowers and the smell of all the different pollens set the aroma of every part of the reception into a good atmosphere. Everyone talking to everyone, all were getting on with each other.

Later in the evening, David and Paula left to go on their honeymoon. They hadn't told anyone exactly where they were going, but it was America. Both sets of parents waved them off as they left for the airport. Both parents received letters from their now new young couple; they had tickets to the top golf tournament, tickets Paula had managed to get from work, and to see the Hoover Dam and Las Vegas. Something Paula had always wanted to do. On their return, both were excited to share their experience with everyone as much as their parents were to show all the wedding pictures, films and videos that had been done nearly a month ago. Paula went a bit overboard with the Hoover Dam experience and Las Vegas was just as she expected. David said, although he didn't like golf, the experience of being there was overwhelming and he would look at golf in a different way from now on. The videos were good and funny in places and the photo album was perfect.

* * *

Good news came when Paula found out she was expecting a baby. David was over the moon and so were the future grandparents. No complications so far, even at work everyone was happy, or so it seemed until, a letter came to him via the internal mail at work. All it said was, 'You may be happy now but it will cost you to stay that way'. Not knowing what it was about he put it in his pocket and forgot about it until a week later when another came with a demand for a personal conference. It was Sandra his workmate! Agreeing to a meeting, he and Sandra went into the office and asked Carol to leave.

"No," was the answer, "I'm staying."

And Sandra said, "Of course you're staying."

David was wondering what this was all about. They both started with, "You remember when you took us to Carol's, when Sandra had a problem with Philip?"

All David could say was, "When?" He had been to Carol's a few times so how was he supposed to remember one time?

"Come round to Carol's tonight and we will show you."

David made an excuse to Paula, he would be late, and went to Carol's house. When he entered, both Carol and Sandra were sitting and asked if he would like a drink.

"No," said David, "just tell me what is happening."

On that they started the video. There was David in his boxer shorts and both girls in their underwear. They looked at David and said, “I’m sure your wife will like to see this.”

On looking at the screen he realised his drink on that night must have been spiked as he could see he was not drunk, just could not help himself to stop doing what they wanted him to do and he didn’t enjoy what he was watching. They said for a fee he could have the tape and they would see him in the next few days.

When he arrived home his wife could see there was something wrong. He was sweating and fidgeting. On being asked, David just came out with everything. Told the whole story about the video and what led up to it. Paula stood by him and said this happened before they met, so whatever happened, drugged or not, take it to the police and let them deal with it. That was a relief for David, his wife on his side. They contacted the police and the following day went to the station to report the blackmail. Having to go to the police station and explain from scratch, right down to the smallest detail, seemed to be a hard task but had to be done.

On entering the police station it seemed small, maybe David had seen too many TV programmes where they seemed much larger. The policeman at the desk asked very politely, "Good morning sir, may I help you?"

David asked, "How do you report someone who is trying to blackmail you, and upsetting your pregnant wife?"

"Just a moment," said the desk policeman, as he picked up the telephone and spoke to another officer.

After a couple of minutes a very smart, well-dressed woman came and requested they go to another room. On entering David was made to feel at ease with a cup of tea and biscuits. He was asked to say a few words, the basic story just for the groundwork to begin. David told of the night visit and the following morning, then the video. The officer asked for names and surnames. When David told her, her eyes sort of opened a little wider as if she were surprised, then she said, "Now we will start from the very beginning of the group to the present day, all visits to houses and anything else as a group, who paid for what etc."

So as to save time the conversation was put on tape and a shorthand secretary also came in to write what was said on tape.

This experience was new. Starting from him arriving in the area and literally putting his life on tape and print. Once started the only time David stopped was for breath, a drink of water or the occasional interruption by the officer just to clarify the last piece of information. It seemed to be over in a flash but the whole procedure took over four hours, to the amazement of David.

Before leaving, the officer said something to David he did not understand. "I think I shall be seeing you sooner than you think," was her comment.

This preyed on his mind all the way home. He mentioned to his wife what the officer had said whilst he also told her what had gone on in the police station. David couldn't get to sleep. He kept thinking of what he had done, what the consequences were, if any, or what repercussions may come from it. The next thing he knew was the ringing of the alarm clock. Paula was already up and when David came downstairs she told him about noticing he wasn't sleeping well lately so left him until the clock woke him. With his toast and coffee there was no conversation but both kept looking at each other smiling. Silence was then broken by Paula asking if he had thought about the comment made by the police officer the previous night. Not really, but he just hoped that everything would be over very quickly.

Going to work David felt uncomfortable. He was sweating as soon as he walked through the door. On arriving at work, the girls asked if he had thought about the night before and was he willing to pay for the video. To their surprise he said no and that he had told his wife the whole story. They looked, and said that was the wrong answer.

* * *

The next few months were the same, David looking over his shoulder and no real communication between himself and the workers. Then one day when Sandra and Carol were about to leave, two policemen and a policewoman turned up and asked if they were the two women in question. On the yes answer, both were cautioned and taken away. As management knew of the situation (the police had to ask permission) the two women were suspended until further notice.

That night sitting at home with his wife watching TV a loud shattering sound was heard. They went to the front room where two large windows had been broken. The bricks that were used had a message on, 'This is for the innocent women you had arrested'. Police were informed but could only say it could be anyone who was a friend of either woman and they would take the bricks to see if they could get a fingerprint but not to be hopeful.

The following day at work, David was snubbed by nearly everyone, no hello, good morning etc. He felt uncomfortable and an hour into the day received a phone call from his wife asking him to come home. A letter was sent to his wife which stated that she had to know everything and not just what had happened. This was going too far for David. Both his and his wife's parents would have to be told before gossip started. Paula's mum and dad asked if she wanted to move in with them for a while until everything settled down. David agreed and Paula put a few things together before giving David a very, very long kiss, then saying everything would turn out okay and she would ring daily.

David rang work to take a few days holiday and he stayed at the house expecting trouble all the time he was there. When the post came it was just a package with a DVD in. On playing it, it was the same as that which he had been shown on video, just transferred and a note which said, 'Everyone you know will receive one of these and your life will be shattered'. Nothing could be done. He had his copy, chances were so did everyone else. To get away from everything he rented out a small place over ten miles away. Nobody knew except his wife whom he told the day he moved. She still loved him and the baby was doing fine. That kept David a little sane. He went back to the house every two days to check the mail and in one was a picture of him and Sandra (from the video) with a note saying that if he was seen in the area there would be trouble.

* * *

Going to see Paula twice a week as well, he kept her informed and made sure she and the baby were in good health. Because of the situation, David had been granted unpaid holiday from work after all his paid holiday had been used, so he had little money coming in. With the police being involved, four weeks later, David received news that Carol and Sandra had been charged with trying to obtain money by blackmail with other charges pending. When it went to court there was a surprise for David, not only were Carol and Sandra there but Philip, John and Charlotte were there as well. It happened that they knew each other before John and Charlotte came to the factory. This had happened before and they had blackmailed other people then left when a few were suspicious before the police were informed. But David let the police know the first day and that was their Achilles' heel.

The court case would last a few days and until it finished David would stay in the flat, where he had been for a couple of months. David had never been in a court before, therefore the surroundings were baffling. Court 1, Court 2, Barristers' Office, Witness Box, Judges' Area etc. He looked lost. Being told where to go and who to meet, David went, sweating heavily.

In the court room, David was sitting with his representative, there was no sign of Carol,

Sandra, Philip, John or Charlotte. He was told they were being kept away and apart from each other, but were in the building in case they were required for evidence. The first day all the jury were sworn in, evidence being read out, who was involved, when, where and whys. This was new to David. Police all around. He was terrified in case something went wrong.

After the first day, David went to his flat but with the pressure of everything, he had let things go downhill. Didn't care about his appearance or the state of the place. Only his wife, unborn child and family. When this case was over and the truth was out, then a new start would be needed, but until then he would look through the blinds from this darkened room with the rain coming down, praying it wouldn't happen again to anyone so the pain and heartache would not be felt by another who tried to help.

The second day was when everyone gave their evidence and a copy of the video was shown to the jury. David had done his bit, listened to everyone else, but was shocked when police from a different area came and gave evidence of the same crime, same offenders, but with no evidence at the time it was kept on file. David went home feeling tired and worn out. He could not sleep, as the result of the case would be tomorrow.

On arrival at court on the third day, he saw his wife Paula, his mum and dad and Paula's mother and father. They all went into court together and waited for what seemed hours before the judge and jury returned. The court found all guilty and sent them to prison for a minimum of five years each. David and Paula held each other as if they were stuck with superglue, Paula crying, David comforting her. Both sets of parents were crying, but now it was all over.

The only other problem was where were Stephen and Emma, Mick and Margaret? They had disappeared as soon as Carol and Sandra were arrested. Were they part of the group or didn't they want to get involved? No one knew, but that thought still haunted David. Time to start again, but not here and with a newborn (nearly), away from anyone who may still think they were not innocent.

Walking away from the court both were still stuck together walking to the taxi. A policeman asked if they were okay and with a big smile both said yes, thanks to the police and justice.